Nelly's Gift

DORENE UNTERZUBER

Trilogy Christian Publishers
A Wholly Owned Subsidiary of Trinity Broadcasting Network
2442 Michelle Drive
Tustin, CA 92780

For information, address Trilogy Christian Publishing
Rights Department, 2442 Michelle Drive, Tustin, Ca 92780.
Trilogy Christian Publishing/ TBN and colophon are trademarks of Trinity Broadcasting Network.

For information about special discounts for bulk purchases, please contact Trilogy Christian Publishing.

Manufactured in the United States of America

Trilogy Disclaimer: The views and content expressed in this book are those of the author and may not necessarily reflect the views and doctrine of Trilogy Christian Publishing or the Trinity Broadcasting Network.

10 9 8 7 6 5 4 3 2 1

Library of Congress Cataloging-in-Publication Data is available.

ISBN 978-1-64773-770-2 (Print Book)
ISBN 978-1-64773-771-9 (ebook)

"We have different gifts, according to the grace given us."

Romans 12:6

It was a bright and sunny morning in the valley. All the insects were awake and busy doing their daily duties. It was a glorious day, and all the bugs were enjoying it—all of them, that is, except Nelly. Nelly was a bit shy, and because she was shy, not many insects paid attention to her. Nelly was also sad. She didn't like the way she looked. She was green—nothing special. She had a lot of legs to get her to where she wanted to go, but they were short and stubby. She thought if she took one wrong step, she'd trip over them and tumble into a ball. How embarrassing that would be! So, she ate leaves and moved from place to place, but that was about it. She was very bored.

One day, she saw a bumblebee float by. Now, *there* was a bug! She was such a sight with her bright, yellow stripes against her flawless, black body.

Nelly sighed. "If only I could be as bright as a bumblebee."

The next day, after climbing through the tall grass, Nelly spied a group of lady bugs. They were very festive with their red wings and black polka dots.

"Very stylish indeed!" stated Nelly, wondering if, one day, green would be what everyone envied.

Nelly continued on and found herself in a bush, munching on some leaves when a praying mantis tight-roped her way past. Nelly stared in awe.

"To be that graceful," Nelly marveled as she took another bite of the tasty leaf.

She looked at her body and realized she was getting very big and very round.

"Goodness! How can I be graceful when I can barely see my feet?" Nelly questioned.

As she walked away from the bush, Nelly saw a line of ants marching as they worked.

"So industrious," Nelly complimented.

The ants worked, bringing food to the colony. Nelly was amazed when she saw an ant lift a crumb of bread as big as his body over his head. It was as if it was only a speck of dust. She saw the ant disappear into his home.

"I wonder what it would be like to be that strong," Nellie pondered as she walked away.

Nelly reached a small stream and gazed at her reflection. All she saw was an ordinary green caterpillar.

"What is so special about me?" she asked her reflection. "I'm not bright or industrious. I'm not graceful or fashionable. I'm just me."

"And what's so wrong about that?" asked a voice.

Nelly turned. "Who's there?"

"It's just me, child," said an old but kind face.

It was Elsie the owl. She was a kind and gentle bird who lived in the valley. Nelly would say hi to her occasionally, but because of her shyness, she never said much more than that.

"Hello, Elsie," Nelly said. "What are you doing here?"

"I came to get a drink from the stream," Elsie replied. "Why are you so sad?"

Nelly looked down at her body, saddened by what she saw. "I don't know. I guess I just wonder what my purpose is. What are my gifts? I see all the other insects, and they know exactly what they are supposed to do. All I do is eat and get rounder and rounder. I'm an ugly green color, and I wobble wherever I go. I guess I don't like what I see."

"Oh, Nelly, your purpose is to serve God," Elsie answered. "He sees what others do not see. He knows everything about you—your heart, your mind, and your soul. Stop looking at what others have and look to what gifts God has blessed you with. Only then will you know what God has specifically planned for you."

"But how am I to know what my gifts are?" Nelly questioned.

Elsie smiled, "God will show you in time."

Nelly thanked Elsie for her time and went on her way. She thought about their conversation all day. *I wonder what gifts God has given me. When will I know when to use them?* Nellie decided to pray.

Dear God, I know I'm not like the other bugs. Please help me to understand why I am different. Please let me see what gifts you have given me and let me use them to do Your will. It's in Your name I pray. Amen.

That night, Nellie felt different. She began to build a lining around herself; it's covering made her feel warm and safe. She fell asleep, and when she awoke, she realized she was changing. Her body became thinner, and her legs were different. She even felt something on her back. Were those wings? She felt scared and yet excited. She knew God was answering her prayer.

Finally, her body stopped changing, and it was time to face the world. Nelly pushed against the cocoon surrounding her. She pushed and twisted, using all the energy and might her body could give. She fought with everything she had in her, using strength she never knew she had. She was about to give up when she saw a sliver of light. She squeezed through the hole she had made, working until she was free from the lining that bound her.

When she was free from the confinement, she gracefully floated to a flower below. As she looked around, she saw the stream and the beautiful butterfly looking back at her.

"Is that me?" Nellie asked.

She turned, and the image in the water turned as well. She moved her wings, and the reflection followed suit.

"It is me!" Nellie exclaimed.

She was stylish with her bright colors and her symmetrical stripes. She was graceful and delicate as she flew to the next sweet-smelling flower. She was industrious, having fought her way out of her cocoon to greet the new day.

She smiled as she thought about the change. *This is what God had planned for me all along, even though I didn't know it. Elsie was right. It's only when we open our hearts to His love that we become transformed. He makes us into the image He had always planned for us. We just need to trust that He will do it in His time.*

Nellie smiled and raised her head to heaven. "Thank You, God, for the gifts You have given me."

"And we know that in all things God works for the good of those who love him, who have been called according to his purpose."

Romans 8:28

CPSIA information can be obtained
at www.ICGtesting.com
Printed in the USA
BVHW020022150521
607436BV00012B/2261